"Be near me, Lord Jesus;
I ask you to stay
Close by me forever,
And love me, I pray."

But sometimes Cindy wondered,
"Where is Jesus? Is He really near me?"

"When my friends came to my birthday party, did Jesus come too?"